OKLAHOMA

The Sooner State

BY
JOHN HAMILTON

Abdo & Daughters
An imprint of Abdo Publishing | abdopublishing.com

abdopublishing.com

Published by ABDO Publishing, a division of ABDO, PO Box 398166, Minneapolis, Minnesota 55439. Copyright © 2017 by Abdo Consulting Group, Inc. International copyrights reserved in all countries. No part of this book may be reproduced in any form without written permission from the publisher. ABDO & Daughters™ is a trademark and logo of ABDO Publishing.

Printed in the United States of America, North Mankato, Minnesota.
052016
092016

Editor: Sue Hamilton   **Contributing Editor:** Bridget O'Brien
Graphic Design: Sue Hamilton
Cover Art Direction: Candice Keimig   **Cover Photo Selection:** Neil Klinepier
Cover Photo: iStock
Interior Images: Alamy, AP, Erin Maxwell, Getty Images, Gilcrease Museum, Granger Collection, Gunter Küchler, History in Full Color-Restoration/Colorization, iStock, Jordan MacDonald, Library of Congress, Lin Harper, Mile High Maps, Mountain High Maps, Oklahoma City Thunder, One Mile Up, RavenFire Media, Red Earth Festival, Tulsa Port of Catoosa, Tulsa Zoo, U.S. Dept of Defense, U.S. Dept of the Interior, Wikimedia.

Statistics: *State and City Populations*, U.S. Census Bureau, July 1, 2015/2014 estimates; *Land and Water Area*, U.S. Census Bureau, 2010 Census, MAF/TIGER database; *State Temperature Extremes*, NOAA National Climatic Data Center; *Climatology and Average Annual Precipitation*, NOAA National Climatic Data Center, 1980-2015 statewide averages; *State Highest and Lowest Points*, NOAA National Geodetic Survey.

Websites: To learn more about the United States, visit booklinks.abdopublishing.com. These links are routinely monitored and updated to provide the most current information available.

Cataloging-in-Publication Data

Names: Hamilton, John, 1959- author.
Title: Oklahoma / by John Hamilton.
Description: Minneapolis, MN : Abdo Publishing, [2017] | Series: The United
    States of America | Includes index.
Identifiers: LCCN 2015957735 | ISBN 9781680783384 (lib. bdg.) |
    ISBN 9781680774429 (ebook)
Subjects: LCSH: Oklahoma--Juvenile literature.
Classification: DDC 976.6--dc23
LC record available at http://lccn.loc.gov/2015957735

CONTENTS

THE SOONER STATE

Oklahoma is a land of great contrasts. There are windswept plains in the west, and green, forested hills in the east. Farmers harvest seemingly endless fields of wheat, while cowboys on horseback wrangle vast herds of cattle. Oil workers pump black gold from deep under the Oklahoma soil. Bustling cities rise from the prairie, making Oklahoma a fast-growing state that is home to many vital industries, including electronics, aviation, and energy.

For much of the 1800s, Oklahoma was known as Indian Territory. It was a place where tens of thousands of Native Americans came to live after being forced off their lands in the East. In 1889, the United States government began opening much of the land to white settlers. During these "land runs," settlers weren't allowed to claim their land until a certain date. Many chose not to wait and staked their claims sooner. That is why Oklahoma is nicknamed "The Sooner State."

The statue "Sacred Rain Arrow" honors Oklahoma's Native American culture. It shows an Apache shooting an arrow into the sky as a prayer for rain.

Longhorn cattle thrive in
Oklahoma's vast grasslands.

QUICK FACTS

Name: Oklahoma is a Choctaw Native American word that roughly means "land of the red people."

State Capital: Oklahoma City, population 620,602

Date of Statehood: November 16, 1907 (46th state)

Population: 3,911,338 (28th-most populous state)

Area (Total Land and Water): 69,899 square miles (181,038 sq km), 20th-largest state

Largest City: Oklahoma City, population 620,602

Nickname: The Sooner State

Motto: *Labor omnia vincit* (Labor conquers all things)

State Bird: Scissor-Tailed Flycatcher

State Flower: Oklahoma Rose

State Rock: Barite Rose

State Tree: Redbud

State Song: "Oklahoma!"

Highest Point: Black Mesa, 4,973 feet (1,516 m)

Lowest Point: Little River, 289 feet (88 m)

Average July High Temperature: 94°F (34°C)

Record High Temperature: 120°F (49°C), near Altus on August 12, 1936

Black Mesa

Average January Low Temperature: 26°F (-3°C)

Record Low Temperature: -31°F (-35°C), in Nowata on February 10, 2011

Low Point: Little River

Average Annual Precipitation: 36 inches (91 cm)

Number of U.S. Senators: 2

Number of U.S. Representatives: 5

U.S. Postal Service Abbreviation: OK

GEOGRAPHY

Oklahoma is in the south-central part of the United States. Colorado and Kansas are its neighbors to the north. Missouri and Arkansas are to the east. Texas shares Oklahoma's southern border. New Mexico is to the west.

Oklahoma is shaped like a giant frying pan, with a long handle sticking out on the western side. This area is called the Panhandle. Cimarron County is in the far western part of the Panhandle. It is the nation's only county that touches four states: Texas, New Mexico, Colorado, and a small part of Kansas.

In total, Oklahoma covers 69,899 square miles (181,038 sq km) of land and water. That makes it the 20th-largest state.

Oklahoma has the most lakes created by dams of any state in the United States. Lake Hefner, named after a former mayor, is a reservoir near Oklahoma City.

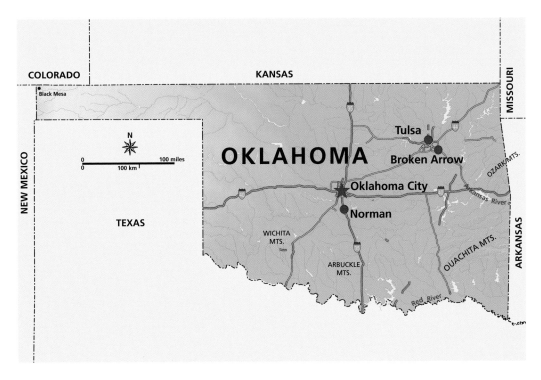

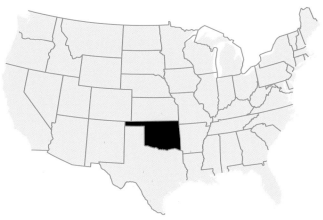

Oklahoma's total land and water area is 69,899 square miles (181,038 sq km). It is the 20th-largest state. The state capital is Oklahoma City.

Oklahoma appears to be mostly flat, but it is actually one big slope. The elevation is highest in the west. The state's highest point is Black Mesa, in the very northwestern corner of the Panhandle. Black Mesa rises 4,973 feet (1,516 m) above sea level. As one travels to the east, the land gradually lowers in elevation. The state's lowest point is along the Little River in the southeastern corner of the state. It rises just 289 feet (88 m) above sea level.

Much of western Oklahoma is a flat, treeless plain that is part of the Great Plains region of the United States. Much of the land is good for cattle ranching, and for growing cotton and wheat. The Panhandle is part of the High Plains region. These grasslands receive less rainfall than the eastern part of the state.

Black Mesa

The Red Bed Plains is a large region that runs through the middle of Oklahoma. There are grassy, gently rolling hills and prairies, with forested areas in the east. Much of the state's oil is found in this region.

There are low mountains and forested hills in eastern Oklahoma. The far-western edge of the Ozark Plateau extends into northeastern Oklahoma. The rugged Ouachita Mountains are in the southeast. Other ranges in the state include the Arbuckle and Wichita Mountains.

Oklahoma has several large lakes, all of which are man-made reservoirs. Major rivers in Oklahoma include the Arkansas, Canadian, and Red Rivers. The Red River forms much of Oklahoma's southern border with Texas.

CLIMATE AND
WEATHER

Oklahoma has a continental climate, far from the moderating effects of ocean currents. That means it has cold winters and hot summers. In July, the average daytime high temperature is 94°F (34°C). The record high temperature occurred near the town of Altus on August 12, 1936. That day, the thermometer soared to 120°F (49°C). The average January low temperature in Oklahoma is 26°F (-3°C). The record low temperature is -31°F (-35°C), which occurred on February 10, 2011, in the town of Nowata in northeastern Oklahoma.

The rainiest part of Oklahoma is in the southeast. That region receives about 50 inches (127 cm) of precipitation each year. The air is humid because of winds blowing inland from the nearby Gulf of Mexico. The driest part of Oklahoma is the Panhandle, in the northwest. It averages about 15 inches (38 cm) of annual precipitation. Statewide, Oklahoma averages 36 inches (91 cm) of precipitation yearly.

Rain and lightning hit an Oklahoma town.

A tornado whirls across rural Oklahoma.

Oklahoma experiences more severe weather than most states. It is in a weather zone called Tornado Alley. On average, twisters whirl over the state about 62 times yearly. Some are very destructive. Only Texas and Kansas are struck by more tornadoes.

CLIMATE AND WEATHER

PLANTS AND
ANIMALS

Today, much of Oklahoma's prairies have been converted to farmland. Some grasslands in Oklahoma are preserved in their natural state. The Tallgrass Prairie Preserve is near Pawhuska, in northeastern Oklahoma. Containing 39,000 acres (15,783 ha) of land, it is the largest protected tallgrass prairie in North America.

Prairie grasses have long roots, which prevent soil erosion. They also provide food and shelter for animals. Some tallgrasses can reach heights of six to eight feet (1.8 to 2.4 m). Common grasses growing on the prairies of Oklahoma include big bluestem, little bluestem, Indian grass, switchgrass, and hairy grama. Cactus, sage, and mesquite are found in the arid Panhandle.

Bison at Tallgrass Prairie Preserve

*The Ozark Mountains cross into eastern Oklahoma from Arkansas. About
28 percent of Oklahoma is covered in forests.*

The official state flower is the Oklahoma rose. The official wildflower
is the Indian blanket, also known as the blanket flower.

About 28 percent of Oklahoma is covered in forests, which is a surprise
to many people. The forests grow mainly in the rainy eastern third of
the state. In the east and southeast are forests of loblolly pine, oak, sweet
gum, and hickory. Piñon pine are found in the northwestern Panhandle.
Other trees in Oklahoma include black walnut, cottonwood, dogwood,
elm, bald cypress, and soapberry. The official state tree is the redbud.

PLANTS AND ANIMALS

Oklahoma's official state animal is the bison, commonly called the buffalo. Vast herds of these large herbivores once roamed the prairies by the millions. Adult males can weigh up to 2,000 pounds (907 kg). Overhunting nearly caused their extinction. Today, small herds thrive in protected areas such as the Tallgrass Prairie Preserve near Pawhuska.

Other animals commonly found in Oklahoma include red and gray foxes, bobcats, badgers, rabbits, and coyotes. Black bears live in the forests of eastern Oklahoma. White-tailed deer live all over the state. Pronghorn are found mainly in the Panhandle region. Many people enjoy spying prairie dogs, although they are not as welcomed by farmers and ranchers. Oklahoma is also home to many armadillos.

A nine-banded armadillo walks across a path in Oklahoma. It is mostly active at night and eats ants, termites, small reptiles, and amphibians, as well as fruits and berries.

Collared Lizard

There are many snakes, reptiles, and amphibians found in Oklahoma, including spotted salamanders, mudpuppies, tree frogs, spring peepers, bullfrogs, snapping turtles, box turtles, and green anoles. The state reptile is the collared lizard, also called the mountain boomer. Venomous snakes found in the state include copperheads, cottonmouths, western diamondback rattlesnakes, and timber rattlesnakes.

Oklahoma has dozens of birds that can be spotted soaring across the prairie skies, or resting on barbed-wire fences. Birds commonly seen in the state include cardinals, woodpeckers, pelicans, egrets, barn owls, roadrunners, red-tailed hawks, bald eagles, pheasants, quail, and greater prairie chickens. The state bird is the scissor-tailed flycatcher.

Fish found splashing in Oklahoma's rivers and lakes include sunfish, bass, crappie, gar, walleye, striper, carp, and catfish. The state fish is the white bass.

PLANTS AND ANIMALS

HISTORY

Prehistoric people of the Clovis Culture arrived in present-day Oklahoma at least 11,000 years ago. They were known for their stone arrowheads and spear tips.

In time, other groups settled the land. People in the wooded, eastern part of Oklahoma built villages and grew crops. On the windswept plains of western Oklahoma, hunter-gatherers survived by following migrating herds of large animals such as bison.

By the 1500s, several Native American tribes had settled into the Oklahoma area. They included the Osage, Apache, Comanche, and Kiowa people.

Native Americans, disguised in coyote skins, hunt bison.

In 1541, the first Europeans entered Oklahoma. They were Spanish conquistadors led by Francisco Vásquez de Coronado. They had left Mexico searching for riches in the desert Southwest. They passed through Oklahoma and made it as far as present-day central Kansas before turning back.

A Spanish Conquistador

During the 1700s, Spain, France, and Great Britain competed for the land, driven by the fur trade. In 1800, France gained control. Just three years later, in 1803, it sold all its lands west of the Mississippi River, including Oklahoma, to the young United States. The sale was called the Louisiana Purchase.

During the 1800s, Oklahoma became a place where the United States government sent Native Americans. Many white settlers were pushing westward and wanted more land. During the 1820s and 1830s, many Native Americans from the southeastern United States either agreed to sell their lands or were forcibly removed by the U.S. Army.

Five of the biggest groups to be relocated were the Choctaw, Cherokee, Seminole, Creek, and Chickasaw people. They were called the Five Civilized Tribes.

Many of the Native Americans were forced to walk to Oklahoma. The 1,000-mile (1,609-km) trek became known as the Trail of Tears. Thousands died along the way.

Tens of thousands of Native Americans from many tribes resettled in what became known as Indian Territory. The land was set aside for Native Americans only, plus some former African American slaves. It eventually was called Oklahoma, which in the Choctaw language means "land of the red people."

Trail of Tears

An Oklahoma land run in 1893.

By the late 1870s, pioneers were demanding that the government allow them to settle in Oklahoma. Much of central Oklahoma was still owned by the government. It was called the "Unassigned Lands." In addition, many Native Americans sold large parts of their lands back to the government or to railroad companies.

The United States finally opened up 2 million acres (809,371 ha) of Oklahoma land to white settlers. To further encourage settlement, it offered much of the land for free. The Homestead Act of 1862 gave 160 acres (65 ha) to anyone who agreed to live there for five years.

On the morning of April 22, 1889, at least 50,000 settlers raced across the Oklahoma border to claim land. More "land runs" took place over the years. In 1907, white and Native American lands were combined and Oklahoma officially entered the Union as the 46th state.

In the 1920s, huge amounts of oil began to be pumped from under Oklahoma's soil. Vast oil reserves were discovered in the area surrounding the city of Tulsa. In the years that followed, oil was found in other areas in Oklahoma. Many landowners became rich overnight. Sleepy towns grew into bustling cities.

An oil well gusher in 1922, in Okemah, Oklahoma.

A dust storm blasts an Oklahoma farm family in 1936.

In 1929, the nation's economy collapsed. The Great Depression lasted well into the 1930s. Oklahoma was hit especially hard. The poor economy happened at the same time as a long drought, which was made worse by poor farming practices. Oklahoma and the surrounding region became known as the Dust Bowl. Wheat crops perished and cattle starved. Prairie winds blew dust everywhere. Many people lost their jobs and their land. Thousands packed up their belongings and moved away. Many migrated to California, hoping to find work. They became known as "Okies."

After World War II (1939-1945), the economy improved. The rains returned, and farmers used better practices to conserve the land. People began returning to Oklahoma.

In the late 1900s and early 2000s, many businesses relocated to the state, including companies in the aviation and air-conditioning industries. These new businesses diversified the economy, making the state less dependent solely on agriculture and oil.

DID YOU KNOW?

• For many people, the only exposure they have to the state of Oklahoma is through the musical stage play *Oklahoma!* Written by Richard Rodgers and Oscar Hammerstein, it tells the story of a cowboy and a farm girl on the Oklahoma frontier. The play had its debut on Broadway in New York City, New York, in 1943. Its catchy songs and energetic dancing have made it a crowd favorite ever since. In 1955, a film version was made starring Shirley Jones, Gordon MacRae, and Rod Steiger. In the title song, the lyrics reflect the optimism of the state's residents, and their attachment to the land:

"OOOOk-lahoma, where the wind comes sweepin' down the plain;
And the wavin' wheat can sure smell sweet, when the wind comes
right behind the rain.
OOOOk-lahoma, Ev'ry night my honey lamb and I, sit alone
and talk and watch a hawk makin' lazy circles in the sky."

The smoldering remains of an Oklahoma African American neighborhood in 1921.

• Before the Civil War, some Native Americans owned African American slaves. When the Native Americans were sent to Oklahoma to live, the slaves came along. After the war, the slaves were freed. Many settled together in towns for self-protection.

During the land runs that started in 1889, more African Americans from the South settled in the "all black" towns. There were 27 towns in all (13 remain incorporated today). Many of the towns were prosperous and vibrant, although they faced racism from their neighbors. In 1921, a race riot raged in a black neighborhood in Tulsa called Greenwood, killing and injuring hundreds of African Americans and destroying 35 city blocks.

• On April 19, 1995, a terrorist's bomb destroyed the Alfred P. Murrah Federal Building in downtown Oklahoma City. Today, the Oklahoma City National Memorial is on the site of the tragedy. It honors the 168 people who were killed, plus the hundreds of others who were injured. The memorial includes massive bronze gates, a reflecting pool, and a field of 168 empty chairs symbolizing those who lost their lives, including 19 children.

DID YOU KNOW?

PEOPLE

Carrie Underwood (1983-) is one of the most popular recording artists of all time. The country music singer and songwriter has won 7 Grammy Awards, 9 American Music Awards, and 12 Academy of Country Music Awards. Growing up in the small town of Checotah, Oklahoma, she sang in talent shows and at her local church. Her big break came in 2005, when she won season 4 of *American Idol*. She released her first album, *Some Hearts*, later that year. It debuted at number one on the *Billboard* Top Country Albums chart. She has since sold more than 65 million records around the world. Underwood was born in Muskogee, Oklahoma.

Ron Howard (1954-) is a successful Hollywood director and producer. He is most famous for his two starring television roles as an actor, as Opie Taylor in *The Andy Griffith Show* and as Richie Cunningham in *Happy Days*. As a director, his most popular films include *Splash* (1984), *Apollo 13* (1995), and *The Da Vinci Code* (2006). He won an Academy Award for Best Director for *A Beautiful Mind* (2001). Howard was born in Duncan, Oklahoma.

Will Rogers (1879-1935) was a writer, stage performer, cowboy, and humorist who helped America laugh during the Great Depression of the 1930s. On stage, he told funny stories while twirling a lasso. He was in dozens of movies, and wrote a newspaper column that appeared in 4,000 newspapers. He once said, "I don't make jokes. I just watch the government and report the facts." Rogers was born in Oologah, Oklahoma.

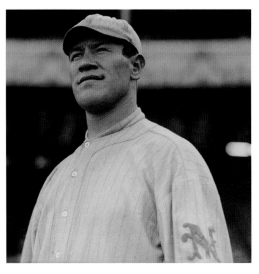

Jim Thorpe (1887-1953) was one of the greatest American athletes of all time. He was born near Prague, Oklahoma, to mixed-blood Native American and European parents. He grew up in the Sac and Fox Nation in Oklahoma. He won two gold medals at the 1912 Summer Olympic Games in Stockholm, Sweden, in the pentathlon and decathlon track-and-field events. He went on to play professional basketball, football, and baseball for several major league teams, including the New York Giants and the Canton Bulldogs.

Ralph Ellison (1914-1994) was one of the most influential American authors of the 20th century. His most famous book was *Invisible Man*. It is about an African American man who believes he is socially invisible to American society because of people's refusal to see him as a full person. The book won the National Book Award in 1953 and was named one of the 100 best novels of the 20th century. He also wrote short stories and magazine essays. Ellison was born and grew up in Oklahoma City.

Woody Guthrie (1912-1967) was a singer, songwriter, and musician. He wrote and sang folk songs about the hardships and hopes of people who lost their jobs and homes during the Great Depression of the 1930s. He learned to play harmonica by age five, and then taught himself to play guitar. He wrote hundreds of songs, including the classic "This Land is Your Land." He was an inspiration to future songwriters such as Bob Dylan, Johnny Cash, and Bruce Springsteen. Guthrie was born in Okemah, Oklahoma.

Sequoyah (c.1765-1843) was a silversmith, and a member of the Cherokee Nation of Native Americans. In 1821, he completed a written alphabet for the Cherokee language. His invention of a practical writing system made it easier for members of his tribe to share ideas and information. Sequoyah was born in Tuskegee, in Tennessee's Cherokee Nation. After relocating to Oklahoma in 1829, he became involved in Cherokee tribal politics.

CITIES

Oklahoma City is the state capital of Oklahoma. It is also its biggest city. Its population is approximately 620,602. The city was founded in 1889. It is located in the central part of the state. It is a sprawling city, covering more than 600 square miles (1,554 sq km). Until the 1980s, the city greatly depended on the oil industry. Today, the economy is much more diverse, with a large variety of businesses. Top employers include state and city government, aeronautics, health care, energy, and telecommunications. There are several universities, including Oklahoma City University, which is well known for its performing arts, business, and science programs. More than 125,000 people each year visit the Oklahoma City Museum of Art and its massive collection of fine art from around the world.

Tulsa is the second-largest city in Oklahoma. Its population is about 399,682. It was first settled by Creek Native Americans in the 1830s. Oil was found in the area in 1901, and the city expanded rapidly. It became known as the "Oil Capital of the World." Oil is still important, but other industries have helped diversify the city's economy. Top employers include aerospace, finance, telecommunications, and manufacturing. Tulsa has a strong arts community. There are many dance troupes, theaters, and concert halls in the city. The Tulsa Zoo opened in 1927. It is home to hundreds of animals representing more than 400 species, including many from Asia and Africa.

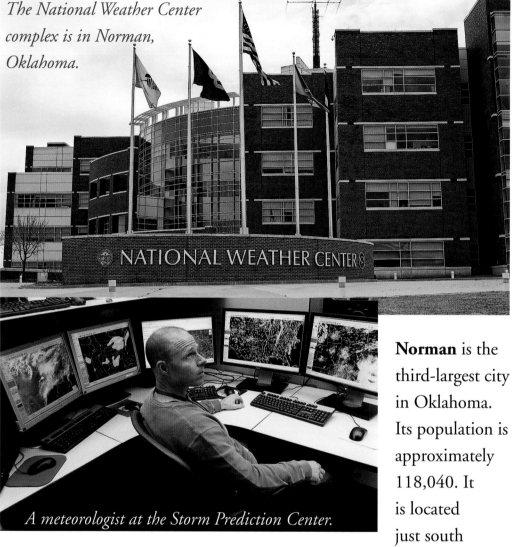

The National Weather Center complex is in Norman, Oklahoma.

A meteorologist at the Storm Prediction Center.

Norman is the third-largest city in Oklahoma. Its population is approximately 118,040. It is located just south of Oklahoma City, in the central part of the state. It was first settled during the Land Run of 1889. Today, big employers include health care, telecommunications, pharmaceuticals, and high-tech electronics companies. Norman is home to the University of Oklahoma, the largest university in the state. It enrolls more than 30,000 students. The National Weather Service operates its Storm Prediction Center in Norman. There are also many museums in the city, including the Fred Jones Jr. Museum of Art, which has nearly 17,000 pieces of fine art in its collections.

An early farm family statue in Broken Arrow, Oklahoma.

Broken Arrow is a suburb of Tulsa, and is the fourth-largest city in Oklahoma. Its population is about 104,726. Founded in 1902, the city is named for a group of Creek Native Americans who had been forced to move to Oklahoma from their Alabama homes in the 1830s during the Trail of Tears. Originally a small farming community, Broken Arrow today is home to many companies that manufacture a wide variety of products, including ice cream maker Blue Bell Creameries. There are many historic buildings in downtown Broken Arrow that the city has preserved.

TRANSPORTATION

Oklahoma has 112,940 miles (181,759 km) of public roadways. Interstate I-40 runs east and west across the state, while I-35 travels north and south. Busy I-44 runs diagonally through the state, from northeast to southwest. All three highways intersect in Oklahoma City in the middle of the state.

Route 66 was one of the first roads built in the United States Numbered Highway System. It opened in 1926. It was a quick way to travel from Illinois to California. Millions of people used Route 66 before it was replaced by high-speed interstate highways. "Get your kicks on Route 66" became a common phrase. Today, many sections of Route 66 can still be driven in Oklahoma.

Bison and longhorn steer statues stand along Route 66 in Oklahoma.

The Tulsa Port of Catoosa is one of the farthest inland river ports in the U.S.

There are 19 freight railroad companies that operate on 3,273 miles (5,267 km) of track in the state. The most common freight carried includes stone, sand and gravel, chemicals, coal, plus food and farm products. Amtrak's Heartland Flyer whisks passengers from Oklahoma City south to Fort Worth, Texas.

The Tulsa Port of Catoosa is one of the farthest inland river ports in the nation. Oklahoma's other major river port is the Port of Muskogee.

The busiest airport in the state is Will Rogers World Airport in Oklahoma City. It handles more than 3.7 million passengers yearly. Tulsa International Airport is the state's second-busiest airport.

TRANSPORTATION

NATURAL
RESOURCES

Oklahoma's most important natural resources are its soil, which is used for agriculture, and the treasures trapped deep beneath the Earth: oil, natural gas, and coal. Throughout most of its modern history, these two industries—agriculture and energy—have been a huge part of Oklahoma's economy.

There are about 78,000 farms in Oklahoma. They occupy 34.2 million acres (13.8 million ha) of land, about three-fourths of the state's total land area. The total yearly market value of Oklahoma's agricultural products sold is about $7.1 billion. The most valuable crops include wheat, hay, corn, cotton, soybeans, and sorghum. Oklahoma is famous for its herds of beef cattle, which number almost 2 million head. Hogs and broiler chickens are other important livestock products.

A rancher checks his cattle in a pasture near Frederick, Oklahoma.

Oklahoma has the nation's fifth-largest supply of crude oil. The state produces more than seven percent of the nation's natural gas supply. Oklahoma also has large deposits of coal. Most of Oklahoma's oil and natural gas deposits are found in the central part of the state. Coal is located in the east.

Forestry plays an important role in eastern Oklahoma's economy. About 65 percent of the state's forests are harvested to make lumber, paper, plywood, and other products.

An oil pump jack works in an Oklahoma cornfield.

INDUSTRY

Oklahoma's workforce totals about 1.9 million people. The number-one employer in the state is government. There are almost as many people working for the federal, state, and local governments (352,000) as there are people in the city of Tulsa (399,682).

Manufacturing is a fast-growing part of the state economy. Oklahoma's factories produce goods such as metal products, tires, tools, equipment for the oil industry, air conditioners, food products, and plastics.

The aerospace industry has been a part of Oklahoma for more than 100 years. The industry employs about 120,000 people in the state. Some of the biggest and most successful aerospace companies operate in Oklahoma, including Northrop Grumman, Boeing, and Lockheed Martin. In Tulsa, American Airlines operates one of the world's largest jetliner maintenance, repair, and overhaul facilities.

Jet engine mechanics work on an airplane engine in the Tinker Aerospace Complex in Oklahoma City, Oklahoma.

An oil refinery outside of Ponca City, Oklahoma. The oil industry is a major part of Oklahoma's state economy.

The service industry represents a large part of Oklahoma's economy. Instead of manufacturing products, service industries sell services to businesses and consumers. It includes businesses such as advertising, financial services, health care, insurance, restaurants, retail stores, law, marketing, and tourism.

Tourism has a big impact on Oklahoma. About 21 million people visit The Sooner State each year, spending $8.9 billion and creating more than 95,400 jobs.

SPORTS

Oklahoma has one major league sports team. The Oklahoma City Thunder plays in the National Basketball Association (NBA). The team began when the Seattle SuperSonics relocated to the city in 2008. The team won its first division title as the Thunder in the 2010-2011 season, and has been a strong contender in the following years. Oklahoma is also home to several minor league professional sports teams that include baseball, hockey, football, arena football, basketball, and indoor soccer.

Many people enjoy watching Oklahoma's college sports teams compete. The schools with the biggest followings are the University of Oklahoma, in Norman, and Oklahoma State University, in Stillwater. Each school has won many national championships in a variety of sports. They both have especially strong football programs.

Boomer is one of the mascots for the University of Oklahoma.

Pistol Pete is Oklahoma State University's mascot.

A rider competes in the bareback bronc division at the International Finals Youth Rodeo in Shawnee, Oklahoma.

Thanks to the state's many cattle ranches, Western heritage is an important part of Oklahoma life. Rodeo is a very popular sport, both high school and professional. Events include bronc riding, steer wrestling, tie-down and team roping, barrel racing, and bull riding. Dozens of rodeos are held each year across Oklahoma.

Oklahomans love outdoor sports, including fishing, hunting, and camping. There are more than 30 state parks spread across the state.

ENTERTAINMENT

There are plenty of things to see and do in Oklahoma, from rodeos and Native American pow-wows to musical theater and fine art museums. Science Museum Oklahoma, in Oklahoma City, features many exhibits that show how science affects everyday life. Its aviation exhibit includes vintage aircraft, as well as the Oklahoma Aviation and Space Hall of Fame.

The Sam Noble Museum is located in Norman, on the campus of the University of Oklahoma. Founded in 1899, it has more than 10 million natural history items in its collections, including dinosaur fossils.

The Red Earth Festival is one of the biggest Native America cultural events in the country. It features elite dancers and artists who compete and perform. The festival opens with a grand parade through downtown Oklahoma City.

The Red Earth Festival is held each year in Oklahoma City in June. It features the skills of thousands of Native American artists, dancers, and musicians.

Artist James Earle Fraser's famous "End of the Trail" sculpture is displayed in the National Cowboy & Western Heritage Museum in Oklahoma City.

The Five Civilized Tribes Museum is in Muskogee. It displays masterpieces of traditional artwork that preserve the history and culture of the Cherokee, Choctaw, Creek, Chickasaw, and Seminole tribes.

The National Cowboy & Western Heritage Museum is in Oklahoma City. For more than 50 years, millions of visitors have toured the museum's large collection of Western art, rodeo photographs, barbed wire, and saddles. The museum also contains three halls of fame, all related to the American West.

TIMELINE

13,000 BC—Prehistoric people of the Clovis Culture arrive in present-day Oklahoma.

1541—The first Spanish conquistadors explore parts of Oklahoma.

1682—France claims a large part of North America, including present-day Oklahoma.

1803—The United States buys land from France. The Louisiana Purchase includes most of present-day Oklahoma.

1820s-1830s—Native Americans from the southeastern United States are forced by the United States government to move to Oklahoma.

1889—The United States federal government opens parts of Oklahoma to white settlers. The first of several "land runs" is held.

1907—Oklahoma becomes the 46th state in the Union.

1930s—The Great Depression and a severe drought strike Oklahoma. The state becomes part of what is known as the Dust Bowl. Thousands of people leave Oklahoma.

1940s—World War II and the post-war economic boom improve Oklahoma's economy.

1995—A terrorist bomb strikes the Alfred P. Murrah Federal Building in Oklahoma City, killing 168 people.

1999—A powerful EF5 tornado touches down for 85 minutes in central Oklahoma, killing 36 people and destroying thousands of homes. The town of Moore, an Oklahoma City suburb, is especially hit hard. The storm becomes known as the May 3rd tornado.

2008—University of Oklahoma quarterback and Oklahoma native Sam Bradford wins the Heisman Trophy. He becomes the fifth Oklahoma Sooner to win the honor.

2013—Moore, Oklahoma, is once again struck by a devastating EF5 tornado. Powerful winds kill 25 people and injure more than 200 others.

GLOSSARY

ARID
A very dry climate.

BISON
A large, four-legged mammal with a humped back. Its front is huge and covered with shaggy fur. Often called a buffalo.

CONQUISTADORS
Spanish soldiers and explorers who came to the Americas in the 1500s. They used force to conquer native people and take control of their lands.

DUST BOWL
In the 1930s, an area of the United States' Great Plains, including the state of Oklahoma, which was over-farmed and then had little rain for several years. High winds swept across the dry land, creating huge dust storms.

GREAT PLAINS
The land east of the Rocky Mountains, west of the Mississippi River and stretching from Canada to the Mexican Border. In its natural state, it is mostly covered with grass, with few trees. Much of the Great Plains today has been converted to farmland.

HERBIVORES
Animals that feed on plants. Cattle and bison are herbivores.

Louisiana Purchase

A large area of land in North America purchased from France in 1803. Today's state of Louisiana was just a small part. The land went from the Mississippi River to the Rocky Mountains and from the Gulf of Mexico to the Canadian border. This land was later split into many new states, including Oklahoma.

Plateau

A large, flat section of land that is raised up from the surrounding countryside. This area of high ground is mostly flat at the top.

Pow-Wow

A Native American social gathering where the people dance, sing, and honor their culture. Pow-wows are sacred events. Many are private, but some are open for the public to observe. Large pow-wows may last an entire week.

Tornado

A violent windstorm. Its main feature is a dark, funnel-shaped cloud that reaches down to the ground. The funnel cloud destroys almost everything in its path.

Tornado Alley

An area of the United States that has many tornadoes. There is no official boundary for Tornado Alley. Many maps show that it stretches from Texas in the south to North Dakota in the north. Some sources say it reaches east all the way to western Ohio.

World War II

A conflict that was fought from 1939 to 1945, involving countries around the world. The United States entered the war after Japan bombed the American naval base at Pearl Harbor, in Oahu, Hawaii, on December 7, 1941.

INDEX